T0146399

the everyman series

being God's man...
by claiming your freedom

Real Men. Real Life. Powerful Truth.

Stephen Arterburn
Kenny Luck & Todd Wendorff

WATERBROOK
PRESS

BEING GOD'S MAN...BY CLAIMING YOUR FREEDOM
PUBLISHED BY WATERBROOK PRESS
2375 Telstar Drive, Suite 160
Colorado Springs, Colorado 80920
A division of Random House, Inc.

All Scripture quotations, unless otherwise indicated, are taken from the *Holy Bible, New International Version*®. NIV®. Copyright © 1973, 1978, 1984 by International Bible Society. Used by permission of Zondervan Publishing House. All rights reserved. Scripture quotations marked (NASB) are taken from the *New American Standard Bible*® (NASB). © Copyright The Lockman Foundation 1960, 1962, 1963, 1968, 1971, 1972, 1973, 1975, 1977, 1995. Used by permission. (www.Lockman.org).

ISBN-13: 978-1-57856-920-5

Published in association with the literary agency of Alive Communications, Inc., 7680 Goddard Street, Suite 200, Colorado Springs, CO 80920.

Printed in the United States of America
2004—First Edition

146646482

contents

welcome to the every man Bible study series

As Christian men, we crave true-to-life, honest, and revealing Bible study curricula that will equip us for the battles that rage in our lives. We are looking for resources that will get us into our Bibles in the context of mutually accountable relationships with other men. But like superheroes who wear masks and work hard to conceal their true identities, most of us find ourselves isolated and working alone on the major issues we face. Many of us present a carefully designed public self while hiding our private self from view. This is not God's plan for us.

Let's face it. We all have trouble being honest with ourselves, particularly in front of other men.

As developers of a men's ministry, we believe that many of the problems among Christian men today are direct consequences of an inability to practice biblical openness—being honest about our struggles, questions, and temptations—and to connect with one another. Our external lives may be in order, but storms of unprocessed conflict, loss, and fear are eroding our resolve to maintain integrity. Sadly, hurting Christian men are flocking to unhealthy avenues of relief instead of turning to God's Word and to one another.

We believe the solution to this problem lies in creating opportunities for meaningful relationships among men. That's why we designed this Bible study series to be thoroughly interactive. When a man practices biblical openness with other men, he moves from secrecy to candor, from isolation to connection, and from pretense to authenticity.

Kenny and Todd developed the study sessions at Saddleback Church in Lake Forest, California, and at King's Harbor Church in Redondo Beach, California, where they teach men's Bible studies. At these studies, men hear an outline of the Bible passage, read the verses together, and then answer a group discussion question at their small-group tables. The teaching pastor then facilitates further discussion within the larger group.

This approach is a huge success for many reasons, but the key is that, deep down, men really do want close friendships with other guys. We don't enjoy living on the barren islands of our own secret struggles. However, many men choose to process life, relationships, and pressures individually because they fear the vulnerability required in small-group gatherings. *Suppose someone sees behind my carefully constructed image? Suppose I encounter rejection after revealing one of my worst sins?* Men willingly take risks in business and the stock market, sports and recreation, but we do not easily risk our inner lives.

Many church ministries are now helping men win this battle, providing them with opportunities to experience Christian male companionship centered in God's Word. This study series aims to supplement and expand that good work around the country. If these lessons successfully reach you, then they will also reach every relationship and domain that you influence. That is our heartfelt prayer for every man in your group.

how to use this study guide

As you prepare for each session, first review the **Key Verse** and **Goals for Growth,** which reveal the focus of the study at hand. Discuss as a group whether or not you will commit to memorizing the Key Verse for each session. The **Head Start** section then explains why these goals are necessary and worthwhile. Each member of your small group should complete the **Connect with the Word** section *before* the small-group sessions. Consider this section to be your personal Bible study for the week. This will ensure that everyone has spent some time interacting with the biblical texts for that session and is prepared to share responses and personal applications. (You may want to mark or highlight any questions that were difficult or particularly meaningful so you can focus on those during the group discussion.)

When you gather in your small group, you'll begin by reading aloud the **Head Start** section to remind everyone of the focus for the current session. The leader will then invite the group to share any questions, concerns, insights, or comments arising from their personal Bible study during the past week. If your group is large, consider breaking into subgroups of three or four people (no more than six) at this time.

Next, get into **Connect with the Group,** starting with the **Group Opener.** These openers are designed to get at the heart of each week's lesson. They focus on how the men in your group relate to the passage and topic you are about to discuss. The group leader will read aloud the opener for that week's session and then facilitate interaction on the **Discussion Questions** that follow. (Remember: Not everyone has to offer an answer for every question.)

Leave time after your discussion to complete the **Standing Strong** exercises, which challenge each man to consider, *What's my next move?* As you openly express your thoughts to the group, you'll be able to hold one another accountable to reach for your goals.

Finally, close in **prayer**, either in your subgroups or in the larger group. You may want to use this time to reflect on and respond to what God has done in your group during the session. Also invite group members to share their personal joys and concerns, and use this as "grist" for your prayer time together.

By way of review, each lesson is divided into the following sections:

To be read or completed *before* the small-group session:
- **Key Verse**
- **Goals for Growth**
- **Head Start**
- **Connect with the Word** (home Bible study: 30-40 minutes)

To be completed *during* the small-group session:
- Read aloud the **Head Start** section (5 minutes)
- Discuss personal reaction to **Connect with the Word** (10 minutes)
- **Connect with the Group** (includes the **Group Opener** and discussion of the heart of the lesson: 30-40 minutes)
- **Standing Strong** (includes having one person pray for the group; challenges each man to take action: 20 minutes)

free—a new kind of man

What is expected of us as Christian men? What are we supposed to do to show our faith in Christ in the real world? We want it spelled out in black and white. Keep it simple. Tell me clearly what I need to do to have a truly authentic and loving walk with Christ.

We often approach our walk with Christ the way we'd tackle a project in the garage: Give me the right tools and plenty of time, and I'll work hard to get it done. In the final chapters of Romans, we'll find the tools to pull off our walk. (For a discussion of the first half of Romans, check out the study titled *Being God's Man...by Walking a New Path.*)

In Romans 12–16, the apostle Paul presented a vivid picture of the godly man in the garage, so to speak, building his faith. It's the picture of a man who has been made new by the gospel of Jesus Christ. He's committed to a life of faith, focused on the Spirit instead of the flesh and now set free to put his faith into action by loving others. No longer consumed with himself and his own needs, he demonstrates his faith by serving others in the most practical ways.

Sadly, few men ever seem to get around to this project. But when a man does commit to putting his faith into action, he enters a new realm of living and experiences a deeper relationship with God. Life begins when a man learns to give his faith away to others. Pity the man who greedily holds on to what was meant to be given away.

Jesus himself showed us a different way to live. In John 13:35, he said, "By this all men will know that you are My disciples, if you have love for one another" (NASB). Our greatest purpose on this earth is to live out the love of Christ in tangible ways, displaying the glory of God and leading others into a love relationship with the One who first loved us. Christ has set us free to exemplify His love in everyday life by giving it away to others. As the apostle Paul said in Romans 13:8, "Owe nothing to anyone except to love one another" (NASB).

Men and women express Christ's love differently. Women tend to empathize and extend comfort while men tend to sympathize and offer solutions. This doesn't mean that men are unable to empathize or are less thoughtful or effective in conveying Christ's love. Nor does it mean that women are "all talk and no action."

A man's way of expressing love isn't any better than a woman's; it's just different. Both ways of expressing love are needed in the body of Christ. Lending a helping hand can be just as significant as extending a caring touch or inviting an encouraging conversation. If I (Todd) know something is causing a friend emotional pain, I immediately want to fix his problem rather than work through its emotional effects. I approach a situation from one angle—"What can I do?"— and my wife comes from a different angle—"How can I help you feel better?" Though our approaches are different, both demonstrate the love of Christ.

Jesus Himself was a man of feeling as well as action. In gospel passages such as Matthew 9:36-38, we see that Jesus had compassion on people and cared deeply for their emotional and physical needs. Sometimes He touched a heart. On other occasions He healed a physical wound. But He always had time for people and expressed love for them in tangible ways. You could see His love for others by what He did for them.

Our goal in this study is to stimulate personal reflection and honest dialogue with God and other men about these matters. As you work through each session, look in the mirror at your own life and ask yourself some hard questions. Whether you are doing this study individually or in a group, realize that complete honesty with yourself, with God, and with others will produce the best results.

Our prayer is that this study will help you walk in Christ's footsteps, demonstrating His love in tangible ways to those around you. May you strive to be God's man in every way by feeling His heart for others and being a conduit of God's good purposes toward them.

risking it all for Jesus

Learning to Surrender

Key Verse

I urge you, brothers, in view of God's mercy, to offer your bodies as living sacrifices, holy and pleasing to God—this is your spiritual act of worship. (Romans 12:1)

Goals for Growth

- Determine what is holding me back from completely surrendering my life to God.
- Strengthen my commitment to complete transformation in Christ.
- Live out a right view of the gifts God has given me.

Head Start

The Christian life is risky. It's like betting all your money on a single stock as opposed to a mutual fund. Instead of spreading out your risk, you put all your eggs in one basket. Jesus did not say, "If a man wishes to come after Me, let him *partially* deny himself, take up *part* of his cross, and *halfheartedly* follow Me." You can't die to yourself halfway. It just won't work.

No. Jesus said, "Deny yourself *totally* and take up the *whole* cross. Risk is involved when you die. But there's no other way. Risk it all and win at the Christian life, or play it safe and lose." Those are the choices every man faces. Too many men today play for the tie, not the win. They hold back from giving the Christian life everything they've got. Is that you?

Risking it all to live for Jesus is called "sacrifice." A sacrifice is always costly and risky. In the Old Testament it meant that one living thing had to die for another living thing. You might be saying, "As long as that living thing isn't me, I'm open."

We figure sacrifice makes for a great man's movie but not for a great life. We all love watching as men march into battle, risking their lives to defend freedom and honor. It's entertaining drama—until *I'm* asked to make the sacrifice!

The point is, God wants me to be a living sacrifice. He doesn't want me to get burned, but He does want me to surrender whatever holds me back from living wholeheartedly for Him. Surrender is costly, but it's always worth it.

"How costly?" you may ask. Let's put it this way: We're way beyond roasting marshmallows. When you roast marshmallows, no one gets hurt. When you die to self, you suffer a painful death. When God uses the word *sacrifice,* He means that the life you used to live is over. It's a new day. It's always for the better, though it may not seem that way in the short run.

One word of caution: The problem with living sacrifices is they have a tendency to crawl off the altar. Since we willingly lay down our lives to become new in Christ, we're free to get up and walk away at any time. It takes a committed man who trusts God's work within him to stay in the flames.

But surrender doesn't stop there. Paul leaves us with a profound paradox: Living sacrifices keep on living. It's one thing to die for Christ, but it's quite another thing—a much more difficult thing—to live for Him. You can't really live until you learn to die.

Connect with the Word

Read Romans 12:1-8.

1. What do you think the expression "in view of God's mercy" means in verse 1? How does God's mercy motivate you to offer your body as a living sacrifice to Him?

2. In the most practical terms, how exactly do you present your body to God as a living sacrifice?

3. Why do you think God considers this an act of worship? When, if ever, have you offered Him this kind of worship? If you haven't, what's holding you back?

4. What is the relationship between being "transformed by the renewing of your mind" (verse 2) and being a living sacrifice?

5. What evidence of mind transformation do you see in your life over the past year or two?

6. Why is it apparently easier to be conformed to the world's pattern than to be transformed?

7. What do you think is the connection between renewing our minds and discovering God's will? How does this help you be a living sacrifice?

8. Do you think men are prone to inflating and exaggerating their view of themselves? Why or why not?

What does it mean to think of yourself with sober judgment? What do you think that looks like in practical terms?

9. How does knowing that you are only one part of the body of Christ and have only some of the spiritual gifts help you have a more humble view of yourself? How does this affect your willingness to surrender yourself to Christ?

10. Carefully review the spiritual gifts listed in verses 6-8. How is your spiritual gift an expression of being a living sacrifice? What evidence do you see in your life that you have been exercising one or more of these gifts? (*Suggestion:* Plan to ask your men's group members whether they can confirm your impressions about your gifting.)

Connect with the Group

Group Opener

Discuss the group-opener questions and the discussion questions that follow. (Suggestion: As you begin your group discussion time in each of the following sessions, consider forming smaller groups of three to six men. This will allow more time for discussion and give everyone an opportunity to share their thoughts and struggles.)

Why do you think we tend to hold back from fully surrendering to God? What are some of the ways we do this?

Discussion Questions

a. What are the differences between being conformed to the world and being transformed by renewing your mind?

b. How do you discern God's will in your life? What's the relationship between knowing God's will and being a living sacrifice?

c. When have you been the most sure of God's will for your life? the most confused or impatient?

d. We discover our spiritual gifts mainly through hindsight. We look back and see where and how God has used us in ministry to others. We get feedback from others about how our attempts at ministry have blessed them—or not. Based on your own past experiences, what do you believe is your primary spiritual gift? (*Note:* See whether the other men respond with an "amen," and ask them, "What gifts do you see working in me?") If you aren't sure what your spiritual gifts are or how to use them, what practical steps can you take to discover them?

e. What is the relationship between being a "living sacrifice" and exercising our spiritual gifts in the church? (*Hint:* The purpose of spiritual gifts is to mutually edify one another and build up the body of Christ.)

Standing Strong

What would you say is the most costly way a man can be a sacrifice for Christ? Explain.

What will it take for you to make this kind of commitment? Jot down the first small step you could take.

Now offer a prayer to God, inviting Him to continue leading you down the path of sacrifice one step at a time.

real men *can* eat quiche

Becoming More Caring

Key Verses

Love must be sincere. Hate what is evil; cling to what is good. Be devoted to one another in brotherly love. Honor one another above yourselves. (Romans 12:9-10)

Goals for Growth

- Be willing to give up my selfish heart.
- Gain a new understanding of how to love others.
- Learn to recognize the needs of others and meet them.

Head Start

During my (Todd's) college days at UC Berkeley in the '80s, I came across Bruce Feirstein's book *Real Men Don't Eat Quiche* while I was studying in the library. At the time I was living in a frat house and playing for Cal's rugby team—and yet I liked quiche. (Our cook in the frat house used to make it regularly.) What man wouldn't like quiche? It's made of eggs, bacon, and piecrust!

I remember thinking, *What crazy meathead wrote this book? What does quiche have to do with being a real man? Eating quiche doesn't make me less of a man!*

Society has been pretty hard on men. It has admonished us to be nicer, more sensitive, less like the traditional "real man" of John Wayne lore. But can't we be both? Isn't a godly man caring and tough at the same time? This is the kind of man the apostle Paul described in Romans 12. According to Paul, God's man cares for others. He's a "spiritual" quiche eater. But above all he sacrifices his life for a cause in which he wholeheartedly believes. He is truly authentic. His words and his actions line up. He's a leader, a servant, a caregiver.

Look at it this way. If quiche had been on the second-century menu, the kind of man Paul described would have dug in. He wouldn't have been embarrassed to reveal a more caring side. Paul calls men to be spiritual quiche eaters while being real men. He presents the image of a mighty man who bridles his power. Such a man isn't afraid to step out of his comfort zone to help others. He is self-controlled and relates to people selflessly. He believes the best about others and offers them grace. He reserves judgment and respects others.

How we treat others mattered to Paul because it matters to God. Romans 12 says that a man who is surrendered to God, transformed by the Word, and committed to serving out of his giftedness approaches relationships differently. There's a caring side to him, and it shows in how he treats those around him. What awesome evidence of the transformed life!

Look at how you treat others and you'll readily see either a transformed life or a life still consumed with self. To find out which applies to you, ask yourself, When confronted with someone in need, what's my first reaction? Do I evade and run? Or do I say, "Tell me more. Let's talk it through. Maybe I can help."

Your gut-level response will tell you whether you're a man who isn't afraid to order quiche from the menu.

Connect with the Word

Read Romans 12:9-21.

1. According to this passage, how are we to behave toward the following people:

believers

nonbelievers

16

2. What kind of person is being described in this passage? Who do you know who most closely approaches the ideal that Paul described in this passage? What do you think is the "secret" of his success in this area?

3. Are these attitudes and actions possible to carry out without being transformed from within by God's Spirit? Explain. What would happen if we tried to behave this way toward others in our own efforts?

4. Which attitude or action is hardest for you to live out? Why?

5. Which attitude or action comes most supernaturally to you? Why? Pause for a moment to offer thanks to God for His work in you.

6. To what degree do you live at peace with others in your daily life (verse 18)? What does your response call you to do?

7. What does it mean to you on a daily basis to "not be overcome by evil, but overcome evil with good" (verse 21)?

Connect with the Group

Group Opener
Read the group opener aloud and discuss the questions that follow.

For a decade Kevin directed the Campus Crusade for Christ ministry on the USC campus. When I (Todd) read Romans 12:9-21, I think of him. No one could outgive, outlove, outcare, or outencourage Kevin. He is the quintessential giver. He believes in everyone. He helps everyone. Spiritually speaking, Kevin is a quiche eater, and he's not less of a man because of it.

There was a lot of crime where we lived near the campus, and I would sometimes see Kevin chasing after a thief who had just stolen something from the dorm or a student's apartment. When Kevin caught the offender, instead taking a baseball bat to his head before going to the police, he'd lecture the guy and then give him another chance at life.

One day Kevin met a homeless man named Dwayne who was living on the streets near Kevin's apartment. Believing the best, he reached out to Dwayne. But Kevin didn't just give him a handful of change; he set up a bank account for Dwayne and helped him find a job. Kevin cared for this guy as if he were a brother. Through Kevin's help, Dwayne restored his relationship with his children and got back on his feet. Even when Dwayne failed and ended up in jail for theft, Kevin was there to encourage him.

Toward the end of that year, Kevin visited Dwayne in the county hospital as he lay dying of cancer. Until the very end, Kevin stood by Dwayne's side, loving him with Christ's love.

Discussion Questions

a. Describe the worst person you can imagine—a guy who's seemingly beyond hope. How do you think God sees that person? What (scriptural) reason would you give for reaching out to him in spite of his sinful condition?

b. What does it take for a man to believe the best about someone who might outwardly show little potential (like Dwayne)? If you've "been there done that," talk about it.

c. Why do men often think loving behavior is too feminine—an exercise in quiche eating?

d. Who do you know who needs to be encouraged or helped the way Romans 12 describes? What could be a first step to take?

e. What does it mean to bless those who persecute us? When, if ever, have you blessed someone who persecuted you? What happened?

f. How has this session helped you redefine your image of a real man?

g. What questions or concerns do you still have about this session's theme? Share one of them with the group.

Standing Strong

What is the most selfless act you could perform this coming week? What steps will you take to follow through?

Ask God to lead you into circumstances that will call for practical, brotherly love.

a new kind of humility

Respecting Authority

Key Verses

Everyone must submit himself to the governing authorities, for there is no authority except that which God has established. The authorities that exist have been established by God. Consequently, he who rebels against the authority is rebelling against what God has instituted, and those who do so will bring judgment on themselves. (Romans 13:1-2)

Goals for Growth

- Recognize all authority as God-given.
- Be willing to submit to those above me out of respect and obedience to God.
- Live as a good citizen with a clear conscience before the Lord.

Head Start

A group of elders gathered to pray, and a most unusual prayer swirled into the heavens. Tim, one of our elders, knelt on the carpet in my (Todd's) office as he began his petition, slowly and deliberately: "Father, help me be a better husband, a better father, a better citizen of my country..."

Naturally, I'd heard the husband and father part before. But not the citizen part. I thought, *Does God really care about us being better citizens?* Yet deep within the heart of Tim's prayer was a truth I'd soon learn to cherish, a truth that shines through in Romans 13.

Think about the sad state our country is in today. A day doesn't go by that we don't hear about murder, adultery, divorce, and political scandals. Does God care if we just check out and let the world go to hell in a handbasket?

I've come to realize that we can't be great men of God unless we're great citizens. That's because citizenship is more than voting, paying our taxes, and obeying the speed laws. It's a matter of changing our whole perspective on authority—on who's the boss and who isn't. Could you stand to grow in that area too? It seems that what God wants to teach us about being men of God starts with living respectfully toward those He's placed in authority over us.

How can that be? For one thing, we are subject to our government not because the politicians necessarily deserve our obeisance or have demonstrated some level of decency that merits our respect. Rather, our submission to earthly rulers teaches us how to submit to the one great President of the universe. Simply put: When we obey our government, we are obeying God. The two go hand in hand. To willingly bow before a representative of God's authority standing there in the flesh of a mere mortal requires a new kind of humility. That humility is hard to find because so often men feel they are above the law. "It doesn't apply to me," we say. "I follow my own conscience." Yet the apostle Paul called men to a higher standard. Godly men humble themselves and live respectfully toward authority, knowing that all authority comes from their Lord in heaven.

Whether you are a Democrat, a Republican, or an Independent, the equation doesn't change. You may disagree with the moral, spiritual, or political beliefs of a particular official, but obedience is still required. God has established authority in our lives to teach us to live under His authority. Godly men submit and live responsibly.

Connect with the Word

Read Romans 13:1-7.

1. What is your usual attitude toward government officials and the mandates of law? toward authority in general?

2. Why do you think God allows corrupt governments and then tells us to obey those He has placed in authority over us?

3. What do you think Paul was trying to say about the relationship between our attitude toward authority and our attitude toward God?

4. In what practical ways is the government a "minister of God" for your good (verse 4, NASB)?

5. How is government good for your conscience (verse 5)?

6. What should our attitude be about paying taxes (verses 6-7)?

7. How does our respect and obedience to our government ultimately affect our relationship with God? (*Note:* Think about how this works out in your own experience.)

Connect with the Group

Group Opener
Read the group opener aloud and discuss the questions that follow.

I (Todd) will never forget the first time I was accused of a crime and stood before a local judge to face the music. A police officer caught me riding my motorcycle on the mountain road above our home. Trouble was, I was only fifteen. Ooops!

My father had given me permission to take my bike up to the radar domes at the top of the hill as long as I walked it to the dirt road. (We were never hassled as long as we weren't on the street.) So I'd laboriously push my motorcycle uphill to the domes.

Since it was an uphill battle, one day I decided to leave the engine on and run alongside the bike as I gave it a little gas. It was a lot easier, and I sure got to the domes faster. Then one day I decided to "ride" the bike, hanging on to one side of the bike with one foot on the pedal. That way if I saw a police car, I could bail off fast. *Technically, I'm not really riding,* I thought.

This worked great. I'd fearlessly cruise all over our neighborhood this way. After many unimpeded trips, I decided to brave the real thing. I hopped on the bike and rode to the domes, right on the street. That's when I got caught.

The day I was to appear before the judge, my father told me to put on my best clothes. As the judge called my father's name, "Theodore Kenneth Wendorff," Dad stood at attention and said, "Yes, Your Honor." When the judge called my name, "Theodore

Fredrick Wendorff," I was whisked to my feet by my father and commanded to say, "Yes sir." I did exactly as I was told.

I learned an important lesson from my father that day: Respect those in authority over me, no matter what. As Christian men set free to live a new life in Christ, our challenge is to learn to respect authority. It leads to the best way of living—with a clear conscience before the Lord.

Discussion Questions

a. When have you "technically" kept the law as Todd did when riding one-footed on his motorcycle? What happened as a result?

b. What are some other ways men approach the command to submit to governing authorities?

c. What is the relationship between obeying the law of the land and obeying God?

d. Do you think you need to grow in your respect for authority? Explain. What specific changes do you think God is calling you to make?

Standing Strong

Think back over your record of conforming to the law. Consider such areas as how you drive, how you pay your taxes, and how you treat officers of the law. What kind of record do you have? In what ways would you like to grow in the coming year as a citizen?

Pray with the men in your group that you will become a more godly citizen and will show the proper respect for those whom God has placed in authority over you.

love—a man's style

Relating Warmly and Giving Practical Help

Key Verses

Let no debt remain outstanding, except the continuing debt to love one another, for he who loves his fellowman has fulfilled the law. The commandments, "Do not commit adultery," "Do not murder," "Do not steal," "Do not covet," and whatever other commandment there may be, are summed up in this one rule: "Love your neighbor as yourself." (Romans 13:8-9)

Goals for Growth

- Gain a new definition of love from a man's point of view.
- Learn new, tangible ways to be loving toward others.
- Let go of unloving attitudes and actions I might have.

Head Start

The TV show *Love, American Style* was a hokey satire on love as it supposedly looked in the USA of the '60s. It portrayed a lovesick culture obsessed with hooking up for long- or short-term romance. Amid the groovy hairdos, wedged sideburns, and bell-bottom pants, the show proclaimed love to be the highest value of our society. That's biblical, but it was a pretty shallow view of love portrayed by some pretty goofy, sex-crazed people.

So how do men view the concept of love these days? If it's not love, American style, then how do we describe it? At the very least, we know that we love differently than women do, and we often feel misunderstood because of it. We even use the word differently. We love pizza and a ball game. We love hanging out with our friends. We love a great movie. We love playing eighteen holes on a Saturday afternoon.

We can also love people. We just show it differently than women, which comes through in the not-so-tongue-in-cheek conversation where the wife asks her husband, "Honey, do you love me?"

"Of course I do, dear," he says. "I told you so on the day we got married! And if I change my mind, I'll let you know."

Obviously, this is a far cry from reality for most of us. I (Todd) would admit that I don't tell my wife I love her often enough. But I've certainly said it more than once since the wedding bells rang.

Yet many of us men *show* our love for our wives through our sacrifice, through working hard to provide what's needed for our family. We work around the house to ensure that our home is a safe haven. We take our wife out for dinner, or we sit around on the couch and listen as she describes her day. That's expressing love too.

We *show* our love for our kids by spending time wrestling with our son or taking our daughter out on a date. We *show* our love for a neighbor by helping him in the garage or by pulling out an old tree stump in the backyard. We *show* our love for strangers by giving them a helping hand in a time of need. For us, it's all about showing the love of Christ by offering a word of hope and extending a helping hand.

I admit that for a guy, *love* is a strange word. We don't quite know what to think of it. Yet men really do know how to love.

It's not love, American style? It's love, a man's style.

Connect with the Word

Read Romans 13:8-14.

1. Paul called on men to be examples of love. Why did he see love as something we actually owe to others (verse 8)? Do you agree? Why or why not?

2. How does love fulfill the whole law (verse 10)? (*Note:* Check out Matthew 22:36-40 before you respond.)

3. How can all the commandments be summed up in one?

4. Why do you think love is more important than all the other commandments? Give a practical example to support your response.

5. In verse 10, Paul mentioned our relationship with our neighbor. Who is our neighbor? (See Luke 10:25-37.) What wrongs do we sometimes commit toward our neighbor?

6. What is the connection between verses 11-14 and Paul's discussion about love in verses 8-10?

7. What effect do the "deeds of darkness" mentioned in verse 13 have on our ability to love others?

Connect with the Group

Group Opener
Read the group opener aloud and discuss the questions that follow.

I (Todd) picked up the phone the other day and heard the voice of a childhood friend I'd known for thirty years. "Can you help me?" he pleaded. "My marriage is falling apart."

As we talked on the phone for nearly an hour, Greg asked, "Do you do a lot of this kind of thing?"

"Yes," I said. "And I'm not the best at it. But I can at least offer you some hope in this troubling time."

I love doing that for others. "You're going to make it," I said to Greg. Then I asked him, "Can I show you what the Word of God has to say about this trial you're going through?"

That's how I help. It's practical, specific, and tangible. There's no need to be afraid of the L word. Any one of us can love another person. But *how* do you do it?

Discussion Questions
   a. How would you answer the last question in the brief story above?

b. On a scale of 1 to 5 (1 = my ability to love is nonexistent; 5 = I eagerly love others in very tangible ways), how would you gauge your ability to love others? What evidence supports your response?

c. In your own life, what does helping-love look like in practical terms?

d. What kind of loving help do most men need from their male friends on a regular basis? To what extent are you receiving this kind of help? To what extent are you giving it?

e. What do putting aside "the deeds of darkness" and putting on "the armor of light" have to do with being a more loving person?

f. What are some practical ways we can love our neighbors in our modern world? What have you tried? What was the result?

Standing Strong

What relational debts do you currently owe others? (Be ruthless with yourself here—think of the love debt you owe your spouse, family, friends, and fellow believers.)

Choose one of the people from your list. What can you begin doing, practically speaking, to clear your relational debts and replace them with acts of love?

helping the weaker man

Staying Strong for the Other Guy

Key Verse

Let us stop passing judgment on one another. Instead, make up your mind not to put any stumbling block or obstacle in your brother's way. (Romans 14:13)

Goals for Growth

- Identify judgmental attitudes I may have toward other men.
- Commit to limiting my personal freedom for the sake of a weaker brother.
- Focus on how I can help build up another man's faith in Christ.

Head Start

Let's face it. Some men are strong, and some are weak. Some can bench-press more than two hundred pounds, while others can barely press fifty. Some men never cry; others cry at the end of *Brian's Song* (the movie about pro football player Brian Piccolo, who died of cancer).

Are you less of a man because you happen to cry when something moves you emotionally? Or are you less of a man because you're not in that great a shape?

What if you are less mature in your faith than some of the other guys? Does this make you less of a man?

The answer is no! You may not be as far along in your faith as others, but that doesn't mean you should feel that you're less of a man.

The apostle Paul set a new standard for men helping other men: The spiritually stronger guy should help the spiritually weaker guy, without judging him. The fact is, when it comes to our faith, we all hold different convictions about moral issues. As Alexander Pope once said, "It is with our judgments as with our watches: No two go just alike, yet each believes his own."

Paul added this crucial spiritual reality: Each of us will have to give an account of himself to God someday (Romans 14:12). So at all costs, don't harm another man's spiritual development. Grab another guy and help him along. Don't force your own convictions on him. Instead, help him develop his own convictions, based on the Word of God. Your watches may run differently, but make sure to pay attention to his watch as well as your own.

Too often we like to prescribe a Christian life ethic for another man without realizing we are all very different. What may work for you may not work for someone else. Each man will be accountable to God for his own actions. Help another guy stand on that day with his head held high because he walked in full integrity before the Lord.

Yes, men have differing convictions about gray areas such as drinking, movies, dancing, and other permissible social activities. In every such gray area—where moral absolutes don't kick in—help another guy make good choices that are right for him, not you. You may disagree with his choices. That's okay. But don't condemn him; help him become a better man before the Lord. "One cool judgment is worth a thousand hasty counsels," said Woodrow Wilson. "The thing to do is to supply light and not heat."

Connect with the Word

Read Romans 14.

1. In your opinion, what does it mean to be "weak in faith" (verse 1, NASB)?

2. According to verses 3-12, what is the basis for determining what you eat, when you worship the Lord, and what you do regarding other ethical and spiritual practices?

3. What are some of the obstacles we can put in a weaker brother's way? When have you seen this happen? What are the consequences?

4. What can you do to personally keep from being a stumbling block to another man? What changes might you need to make in your beliefs or attitudes to avoid doing this?

5. Verses 22 and 23 seem to indicate that each man will grow stronger as his faith develops. What can a man do to grow in faith so that his convictions match what the Word of God teaches?

Connect with the Group

Group Opener
Read the group opener aloud and discuss the questions that follow.

While I (Todd) was at UC Berkeley, the rugby team's motto was "Rugby players drink more beer." I always wondered, *More beer than whom? More than my fraternity brothers?* I think that contest would have ended in a tie.

During those years I was being mentored by an older, wiser Christian man. His name was John Bruce. John never judged me for living in that environment. He never laid down "the rules." He only challenged me to grow strong in my faith in the Lord. He wasn't worried about my morality as much as he cared about my spiritual development, because he knew that one would follow the other. Week after week I'd meet with John, and he'd always ask me the same question: "What are you learning in the Word this week?" After a while it became apparent that we weren't going to trade opinions; we were going to exchange insights into God's Word.

Too often we make the kingdom of God all about eating and drinking when it's really all about righteousness, peace, and joy in the Holy Spirit. Ultimately, if we fail to develop a walk of faith, we fail to nurture the moral convictions that act as our compass in life. In Proverbs 4:5-6, wisdom is personified as a cherished possession because of what it will accomplish in our lives: "Get wisdom, get understanding; do not forget my words or swerve from them. Do not forsake wisdom, and she will protect you; love her, and she will watch over you." The apostle Paul encourages us not to judge another guy but to help him walk the walk of faith, to build the biblical foundation upon which his personal and moral convictions will stand strong.

Discussion Questions

a. In what unsavory environment have you found yourself living? How did that atmosphere affect your spiritual growth?

b. Do you agree that we tend to make the kingdom of God all about rules and behaviors? Why or why not? In Paul's day, eating, drinking, and worship were the contentious issues. What are the key issues for us today?

c. According to the apostle Paul, in what practical ways can grace confront our legalistic tendencies to judge others? (Look at Romans 14:15-21 for clues.)

d. Do you consider yourself spiritually weak or spiritually strong? Why?

e. What do you think Paul meant when he said, "He who eats… eats to the Lord" (verse 6)? According to this verse, what is the key factor in determining whether or not you should do a certain thing?

f. How can we help another guy develop convictions that line up with the Word of God? Be as specific as possible.

Standing Strong

Identify a man you might be able to help this week. Write his initials here: _____. What kind of help do you think he needs? In what ways could you limit your own freedom for his sake?

"i've got your back"

Helping a Brother Grow

Key Verse

We who are strong ought to bear with the failings of the weak and not to please ourselves. (Romans 15:1)

Goals for Growth

- Evaluate my level of spiritual maturity, and pursue growth in the areas where I'm weakest.
- Consider how to help other men become more mature in their faith.
- Learn how to encourage a weaker brother in practical ways.

Head Start

One year The Power Team came to our city and performed at a local church. My (Todd's) son was especially impressed with the strength of these men. He loved watching them bend steel, rip telephone books in half, crush cans with their foreheads, and clean and jerk telephone poles on stage. What a show! Then they shared the gospel, explaining how we can have power through Christ alone.

I remember thinking, *These guys are strong. They have muscles I never thought existed.*

It's one thing to be strong physically, but what about being spiritually strong? To be strong in the Lord, we need to grow and mature in the faith "until we all attain to the unity of the faith, and of the knowledge of the Son of God, to a mature man, to the measure of the stature which belongs to the fullness of Christ.… We are to grow up in all aspects into Him who is the head, even Christ" (Ephesians 4:13,15, NASB).

That's our goal: to grow up and be like Jesus. And just as those Power Team men spent countless hours in rigorous workouts and weight training, we need to train hard to grow spiritually. In Ephesians 6:10, Paul said, "Be strong in the Lord and in his mighty power."

"Be strong." Yet not all of us are. Many men are weak in their faith. They've focused their attention on other matters. They're strong in sports, strong in their jobs, strong in their negotiating skills, strong in their financial prowess, but they're not strong in the things of God. They cover up their spiritual weakness by not entering into the daily battle for their faith.

Physically, we are all built differently. Some of us are a little pudgier around the middle than others—some guys look like Olympic athletes, while others look more like novice thumb wrestlers. And we're all at different stages of spiritual development.

Here's the point: The apostle Paul tells the stronger men to help the weaker men. If you are further along in your faith than other men you know, help them out. Paul says, "build them up." He says our strength comes not from the weight room but from understanding the Scriptures and from the power of the Holy Spirit. (See Romans 15:4,13.)

As you grow deeper in your knowledge of the Word and rely on the power of the Holy Spirit, you will become strong and mature in the faith. And as you grow, bring a weaker guy along with you.

Connect with the Word

Read Romans 15:1-13.

1. In light of this passage, what factors seem to determine a man's spiritual strength?

2. How do the following factors contribute to a man's strength?

the Scriptures (verse 4)

being of the same mind (verse 5, NASB)

accepting one another (verse 7)

the power of the Holy Spirit (verse 13)

3. In what ways can a stronger man help a weaker man, practically speaking (verses 1,2,5,7,8)? How would this look in your world?

4. Paul encourages us to "be of the same mind with one another" (verse 5, NASB). How can we do this if some of us are stronger in our faith than others?

5. We are not to judge or condemn the weaker brother; rather, we should help him out. (See verses 2 and 7.) If we were to live this out, do you think our approach to others would change from a competitive one to a more cooperative and sacrificial one? Explain.

Connect with the Group

Group Opener
Read the group opener aloud and discuss the questions that follow.

As The Power Team performed, it was obvious that not all the members of the team had equal strength. Not all were good at the same thing. Each of them had special talents. Some could bend steel, while others could clean and jerk a telephone pole. They each had their moment of fame and received applause from the audience as they performed their specialty.

What was interesting to me (Todd) was how they helped each other out. There were spotters and encouragers for each of the stunts. No man was alone in his performance.

One of the athletes was a young man who had grown up watching The Power Team perform. He described himself as a scrawny little kid who knew he didn't have the height or the strength to ever join the team. Yet he was determined to be a member one day.

That day finally arrived. As he performed on stage, his teammates, who were obviously stronger and bigger than he, helped him through his routine, offering encouragement and assistance. He became a Power Team member not on his own but with the help of the other members of the team.

The point: Rather than just looking out for number one, pay attention to other guys who need a little encouragement to grow. The apostle Paul encourages us to be aware of others' needs so we can offer a helping hand at just the right time.

Discussion Questions

a. In what ways is your men's group like The Power Team? What is the ultimate challenge for your team right now?

b. Evaluate your spiritual maturity on a scale of 1 to 5
(1 = immature; 5 = confident in your walk with the Lord).
Then ask the other guys for their input.

c. In light of Romans 15:1-13, what might be some practical ways to strengthen your faith?

d. How are we to treat someone who is weaker in faith than we are? When, if ever, have you seen this principle in action? Talk about it.

e. What do you think is the intended goal of helping the weaker brother? (See verses 2, 5, and 13.)

Standing Strong

List some of the ways you plan to strengthen your faith in the coming months.

Name a friend who you feel needs some encouragement in his faith. List some ways you plan to help this brother in Christ.

show it!

Committing Acts of Kindness Toward Unbelievers

Key Verse

Therefore I glory in Christ Jesus in my service to God. (Romans 15:17)

Goals for Growth

- Consider how I'm "spending" my life.
- Become more aware of the needs around me.
- Identify specific acts of kindness I could do for others.

Head Start

In the fall of 2003, four independent fires raged through the Los Angeles area, with nearly three hundred thousand acres succumbing to the flames. One of the fires reached Valley Center, leaving scores of homes and families devastated. Those who lost their homes had no fallback position. Two families lost a loved one in the fire.

On the Saturday following "containment" of the fire, the men of Ridgeview Church decided to help out. Instead of heading to the mountains for their annual men's retreat, they stayed in Valley Center and spent the day cleaning scorched homes. Then the ensuing rains brought another kind of damage to the properties: erosion caused by flooding and mud slides. The men stayed to help with that, too. It was the clearest demonstration of Christ's love I (Todd) have ever seen. More than one hundred men donated to this desperate community about a thousand man-hours and thousands of dollars' worth of supplies, equipment, and skill.

Like the men of Ridgeview Church, the apostle Paul always kept in mind the physical needs of the people he was inviting into God's family. He knew that if he wanted to be an effective ambassador of God's grace, he needed to apply it to every area of people's lives, including meeting their physical needs.

All too often our own witness for Christ is expressed in words alone. Lots of words; little action. Don't we know that our strongest testimony to God's generous love is our own generous outpouring of practical help to others? We make the greatest impact for Christ when our words come packaged with deeds. Unbelievers not only need to hear about Jesus's love for them; they need to feel that love as well!

The people of Valley Center responded with profound gratitude for the help they received from the men of Ridgeview Church that Saturday after the fire. But Sunday morning said it all. Ridgeview Church was packed and filled with excitement. And over the coming weeks, many in the community kept coming back to learn more about Christ's awesome love for them.

There are so many ways we can spend our lives. We can spend them building our careers. We can spend them on a very fulfilling hobby that becomes all-consuming. Or we can spend our lives investing in the lives of others with our words and deeds. The eternal rewards we'll receive by investing in others will far outweigh the temporary pleasures of living for ourselves.

What will you do to reach out to those who so clearly need God's touch?

Connect with the Word

Read Romans 15:14-33.

1. What did Paul find worthy of glorying in (verses 17-18)? How did this keep him focused on his mission in life?

2. What kinds of things do men tend to glory in? How do these things keep us from living out our mission in life?

3. According to verse 18, what kinds of things do you think Paul spoke about that caused others to turn to Christ? What might that look like for you where you live and work?

4. God showed that He was working through Paul by signs and miracles and the display of the Holy Spirit's power (verse 19). In what ways, if any, has God displayed His miraculous power through you in the lives of others? How are these examples of "showing" your faith rather than just "telling" it?

5. How can men today "fully [proclaim] the gospel of Christ" (verse 19)? In your opinion, is it possible to do this without offending the so-called politically correct sensitivities of our day? Explain.

jections, and liposuction or diet pills for rapid weight loss. So when it comes to spiritual growth, we naturally expect instant faithfulness to the Lord rather than viewing it as a long-term project. But I (Todd) have learned an important truth about the Christian life from the lives of believers in the Bible: It's not how you start that counts; it's how you finish. And finishing well takes time.

Whenever my wife, Denise, wants more done around the house, I respond, "One project at a time, honey." That's a good motto for the Christian life as well. Our problem is that we want everything fixed *right now*. We want instant spiritual maturity. With one magical jolt, we want to rid ourselves of our sin issues and become caring, helpful men *today*. We want to clean up all our bothersome personality quirks, irritating habits, and self-destructive addictions so we can present ourselves to the Lord as perfectly spotless little lambs for His glory. "Isn't it wonderful, Jesus, what I've done with myself?"

But we don't have the power to transform ourselves. It's God's work, and He will take His own precious time molding us into the kind of men He wants us to be. Time is essential because we're slow learners. But God knows that and willingly accommodates us. He loves us that much.

At the end of his letter to the Romans, the apostle Paul recognized by name all the faithful believers who had stayed the course in their walk with Christ. They didn't burn out or rust out. They lived out their faith over the long haul. They finished strong, and they finished well. Paul commended several of them for their hard work in the Lord.

What is God attempting to do in your life right now? Are you frustrated or impatient with your progress? Do you find yourself wanting to proclaim success too soon? Chill out and give God time to finish the work He's doing in your life. Remember that "he who began a good work in you will carry it on to completion until the day of Christ Jesus" (Philippians 1:6).

Connect with the Word

Read Romans 16.

1. Look at all the names of the believers Paul mentioned in this chapter. Why do you think these fellow believers meant so much to Paul?

2. What clues does Paul give us about the faithfulness of these believers and their ability to stand strong for Christ over the long haul (verses 12,17,19)?

3. How could divisions and obstacles, caused by those who have fallen away, affect your ability to be faithful over the long haul (verse 17)? Why do you think Paul cautions us to keep away from people like this?

4. In considering how to finish well, what do you think it means to be "wise about what is good and innocent about what is evil" (verse 19)?

5. What steps can you take to become more aware of people and things that are destructive to your faith and steer clear of them (verses 17-19)?

6. In light of this passage, what do you think it takes to be faithful to God over the long haul? (Be sure to name some of the particular issues that make it difficult for you personally.)

7. What is God's role in helping you finish well (verses 20,25-27)?

Connect with the Group

Group Opener
Read the group opener aloud and discuss the questions that follow.

My wife and I (Todd) recently bought a fixer-upper house. My wife calls it the Sloping Blue Manor. The experience has been a real downer for both of us. Built in the '50s, the house has needed more than just a new paint job and a few shelves installed in the living room.

First, everything was powder blue—the outside, the inside, the tile on the floor, the kitchen cabinets, even the walls. We are not blue people. Second, the house sits on a slope and has settled a bit. Yet it was the only affordable house in the community where we want to live.

After closing escrow, we tore out walls, put in a new kitchen and great room, installed new doors and windows, added two bedrooms, and painted the entire house (obviously not blue).

My personal recommendation? Don't ever try rennovating a house all at once. We went too fast and wore ourselves out. And we're still not done. Baseboards need to be installed, the front entry needs to be grouted, the deck railing is missing, and a million other small details cry out for more manual labor.

But we'll get there. We've done projects like this before. But it takes time. *Lots* of time. Kind of like spiritual growth. Spiritual maturity doesn't happen overnight; it's a lifelong endeavor. But God does promise to finish it up.

Discussion Questions

a. In what ways can you relate to the fixer-upper challenge? Do you think the Lord views our lives that way? Why or why not?

b. When it comes to spiritual growth, why do many men seek instant results, become frustrated with the process of change, and end up settling for less? What is your experience with this?

c. Share your response to the final question in Connect with the Word. What progress are you making on the issues you listed? How can the guys in your group pray for you concerning these issues?

d. Romans 16:12 says that some of the believers who helped Paul worked "hard." In Greek this literally means "to toil to the point of exhaustion." In what practical ways can you work that hard at your faith?

e. In light of Romans 16 (especially verses 20-27), what is the role of God's grace in our spiritual growth? How would you explain the apparent paradox that spiritual growth is a result of both God's unconditional grace and our own hard work? (See Philippians 2:12.)

Standing Strong

What specific steps do you plan to take to remain faithful to the Lord over the long haul? What might it look like for you to work hard at growing in your faith?

6. How did Paul, along with others, show his faith (verses 25-27)?

7. Our witness for Christ flows out of how we relate to one another. According to verses 30-33, what shows Christ's love to others?

Connect with the Group

Group Opener
Discuss the group-opener questions and the discussion questions that follow.

Would you say you are better at telling others the gospel message or showing it through acts of kindness? What evidence supports your response?

Discussion Questions

a. List some practical ways men can show the love of Christ to others.

b. What, in your opinion, are some of the most effective ways men can talk about Jesus? What principles would you suggest for being inviting and winsome in your verbal witness rather than turning people off?

c. In Romans 15:16, Paul called himself a "minister of Christ Jesus." What do you think it would look like for a man to be a minister when he works sixty-plus hours per week at a job?

d. In Romans 15:26-27, Paul referred to the Gentile churches that helped the Jewish churches back in Jerusalem. Nonbelievers must have been impressed by this display of Christian concern. In what specific ways can we help one another so that non-believers will see the love of Christ in action?

Standing Strong

Identify a few acts of kindness that you will commit to doing for a nonbelieving friend, neighbor, or co-worker this week.

finishing well, finishing strong

Living Faithfully over the Long Haul

Key Verses

Greet Tryphena and Tryphosa, those women who work hard in the Lord. Greet my dear friend Persis, another woman who has worked very hard in the Lord. Greet Rufus, chosen in the Lord, and his mother, who has been a mother to me, too. (Romans 16:12-13)

Goals for Growth

- Commit to being faithful to the Lord over the long haul.
- Identify areas in my life that still need the Spirit's work.
- Stay clear of deception and evil desires that hinder my spiritual growth.

Head Start

We've become a culture enamored with instant results and quick fixes—fast food, instant mashed potatoes, hair implants, botox in-

d. Romans 16:12 says that some of the believers who helped Paul worked "hard." In Greek this literally means "to toil to the point of exhaustion." In what practical ways can you work that hard at your faith?

e. In light of Romans 16 (especially verses 20-27), what is the role of God's grace in our spiritual growth? How would you explain the apparent paradox that spiritual growth is a result of both God's unconditional grace and our own hard work? (See Philippians 2:12.)

Standing Strong

What specific steps do you plan to take to remain faithful to the Lord over the long haul? What might it look like for you to work hard at growing in your faith?

Discussion Questions

a. In what ways can you relate to the fixer-upper challenge? Do you think the Lord views our lives that way? Why or why not?

b. When it comes to spiritual growth, why do many men seek instant results, become frustrated with the process of change, and end up settling for less? What is your experience with this?

c. Share your response to the final question in Connect with the Word. What progress are you making on the issues you listed? How can the guys in your group pray for you concerning these issues?

Connect with the Group

Group Opener

Read the group opener aloud and discuss the questions that follow.

My wife and I (Todd) recently bought a fixer-upper house. My wife calls it the Sloping Blue Manor. The experience has been a real downer for both of us. Built in the '50s, the house has needed more than just a new paint job and a few shelves installed in the living room.

First, everything was powder blue—the outside, the inside, the tile on the floor, the kitchen cabinets, even the walls. We are not blue people. Second, the house sits on a slope and has settled a bit. Yet it was the only affordable house in the community where we want to live.

After closing escrow, we tore out walls, put in a new kitchen and great room, installed new doors and windows, added two bedrooms, and painted the entire house (obviously not blue).

My personal recommendation? Don't ever try rennovating a house all at once. We went too fast and wore ourselves out. And we're still not done. Baseboards need to be installed, the front entry needs to be grouted, the deck railing is missing, and a million other small details cry out for more manual labor.

But we'll get there. We've done projects like this before. But it takes time. *Lots* of time. Kind of like spiritual growth. Spiritual maturity doesn't happen overnight; it's a lifelong endeavor. But God does promise to finish it up.

4. In considering how to finish well, what do you think it means to be "wise about what is good and innocent about what is evil" (verse 19)?

5. What steps can you take to become more aware of people and things that are destructive to your faith and steer clear of them (verses 17-19)?

6. In light of this passage, what do you think it takes to be faithful to God over the long haul? (Be sure to name some of the particular issues that make it difficult for you personally.)

7. What is God's role in helping you finish well (verses 20,25-27)?

wanting to proclaim success too soon? Chill out and give God time to finish the work He's doing in your life. Remember that "he who began a good work in you will carry it on to completion until the day of Christ Jesus" (Philippians 1:6).

Connect with the Word

Read Romans 16.

1. Look at all the names of the believers Paul mentioned in this chapter. Why do you think these fellow believers meant so much to Paul?

2. What clues does Paul give us about the faithfulness of these believers and their ability to stand strong for Christ over the long haul (verses 12,17,19)?

3. How could divisions and obstacles, caused by those who have fallen away, affect your ability to be faithful over the long haul (verse 17)? Why do you think Paul cautions us to keep away from people like this?

jections, and liposuction or diet pills for rapid weight loss. So when it comes to spiritual growth, we naturally expect instant faithfulness to the Lord rather than viewing it as a long-term project. But I (Todd) have learned an important truth about the Christian life from the lives of believers in the Bible: It's not how you start that counts; it's how you finish. And finishing well takes time.

Whenever my wife, Denise, wants more done around the house, I respond, "One project at a time, honey." That's a good motto for the Christian life as well. Our problem is that we want everything fixed *right now*. We want instant spiritual maturity. With one magical jolt, we want to rid ourselves of our sin issues and become caring, helpful men *today*. We want to clean up all our bothersome personality quirks, irritating habits, and self-destructive addictions so we can present ourselves to the Lord as perfectly spotless little lambs for His glory. "Isn't it wonderful, Jesus, what I've done with myself?"

But we don't have the power to transform ourselves. It's God's work, and He will take His own precious time molding us into the kind of men He wants us to be. Time is essential because we're slow learners. But God knows that and willingly accommodates us. He loves us that much.

At the end of his letter to the Romans, the apostle Paul recognized by name all the faithful believers who had stayed the course in their walk with Christ. They didn't burn out or rust out. They lived out their faith over the long haul. They finished strong, and they finished well. Paul commended several of them for their hard work in the Lord.

What is God attempting to do in your life right now? Are you frustrated or impatient with your progress? Do you find yourself

small-group resources

leader tips

What if men aren't doing the Connect with the Word section before our small-group session?

Don't be discouraged. You set the pace. If you are doing the study and regularly referring to it in conversations with your men throughout the week, they will pick up on its importance. Here are some suggestions to motivate the men in your group to do their home Bible study:

- Send out a midweek e-mail in which you share your answer to one of the study questions. This shows them that you are personally committed to and involved in the study.
- Ask the guys to hit "respond to all" on their e-mail program and share one insight from that week's Bible study with the entire group. Encourage them to send it out before the next small-group session.
- Every time you meet, ask each man in the group to share one insight from his home study.

What if men are not showing up for small group?

This might mean they are losing a sin battle and don't want to admit it to the group. Or they might be consumed with other priorities. Or maybe they don't think they're getting anything out of the group. Here are some suggestions for getting the guys back each week:

- Affirm them when they show up, and tell them how much it means to you that they make small group a priority.

- From time to time, ask them to share one reason small group is important to them.
- Regularly call or send out an e-mail the day before you meet to remind them you're looking forward to seeing them.
- Check in with any guy who has missed more than one session and find out what's going on in his life.
- Get some feedback from the men. You may need to adjust your style. Listen and learn.

What if group discussion is not happening?

You are a discussion facilitator. You have to keep guys involved in the discussion or you'll lose them. You can engage a man who isn't sharing by saying, "Chuck, you've been quiet. What do you think about this question or discussion?" You should also be prepared to share your own personal stories that are related to the discussion questions. You'll set the example by the kind of sharing you do.

What if one man is dominating the group time?

You have to deal with it. If you don't, men will stop showing up. No one wants to hear from just one guy all the time. It will quickly kill morale. Meet with the guy in person and privately. Firmly but gently suggest that he allow others more time to talk. Be positive and encouraging, but truthful. You might say, "Bob, I notice how enthusiastic you are about the group and how you're always prepared to share your thoughts with the group. But there are some pretty quiet guys in the group too. Have you noticed? Would you be willing to help me get them involved in speaking up?"

How do I get the guys in my group more involved?

Give them something to do. Ask one guy to bring a snack. Invite another to lead the prayer time (ask in advance). Have a guy sub for you one week as the leader. (Meet with him beforehand to walk through the group program and the time allotments for each segment.) Encourage another guy to lead a subgroup.

What if guys are not being vulnerable during the Standing Strong or prayer times?

You model openness. You set the pace. Honesty breeds honesty. Vulnerability breeds vulnerability. Are you being vulnerable and honest about your own problems and struggles? (This doesn't mean that you have to spill your guts each week or reveal every secret of your life.) Remember, men want an honest, on-their-level leader who strives to walk with God. (Also, as the leader, you need an accountability partner, perhaps another group leader.)

What will we do at the first session?

We encourage you to open by discussing the **Small-Group Covenant** we've included in this resource section. Ask the men to commit to the study, and then discuss how long it will take your group to complete each session. (We suggest 75-90 minute sessions.) Men find it harder to come up with excuses for missing a group session if they have made a covenant to the other men right at the start.

Begin to identify ways certain men can play a more active role in small group. Give away responsibility. You won't feel as burdened, and your men will grow from the experience. Keep in mind that this process can take a few weeks. Challenge men to fulfill one of the group roles identified later in this resource section. If no one steps forward to fill a role, say to one of the men, "George, I've noticed that you are comfortable praying in a group. Would you lead us each week during that time?"

How can we keep the group connected after we finish a study?
Begin talking about starting another Bible study before you finish this eight-week study. (There are several other studies to choose from in the Every Man Bible study series.) Consider having a social time at the conclusion of the study, and encourage the men to invite a friend. This will help create momentum and encourage growth as you launch into another study with your group. There are probably many men in your church or neighborhood who aren't in small groups but would like to be. Be the kind of group that includes others.

As your group grows, consider choosing an apprentice leader who can take half the group into another room for the **Connect with the Group** time. That subgroup can stay together for prayer, or you can reconvene as a large group during that time. You could also meet for discussion as a large group and then break into subgroups for **Standing Strong** and **prayer.**

If your group doubles in size, it might be a perfect opportunity to release your apprentice leader with half the group to start another group. Allow men to pray about this and make a decision as a group. Typically, the relational complexities that come into play when a small group births a new group work themselves out. Allow guys to choose which group they'd like to be a part of. If guys are slow in choosing one group or another, ask them individually to select one of the groups. Take the lead in making this happen.

Look for opportunities for your group to serve in the church or community. Consider a local outreach project or a short-term missions trip. There are literally hundreds of practical ways you can serve the Lord in outreach. Check with your church leaders to learn the needs in your congregation or community. Create some interest by sending out scouts who will return with a report for the group. Serving keeps men from becoming self-focused and ingrown. When you serve as a group, you will grow as a group.

using this study in a large-group format

Many church leaders are looking for biblically based curriculum that can be used in a large-group setting, such as a Sunday-school class, or for small groups within an existing larger men's group. Each of the Every Man Bible studies can be adapted for this purpose. In addition, this curriculum can become a catalyst for churches wishing to launch men's small groups or to build a men's ministry.

Getting Started

Begin by getting the word out to men in your church, inviting them to join you for a men's study based on one of the topics in the Every Man Bible study series. You can place a notice in your church bulletin, have the pastor announce it from the pulpit, or pursue some other means of attracting interest.

Orientation Week

Arrange your room with round tables and chairs. Put approximately six chairs at each table.

Start your session in prayer and introduce your topic with a short but motivational message from any of the scriptures used in the Bible study. Hand out the curriculum and challenge the men to do their homework before each session. During this first session give the men some discussion questions based upon an overview of the material and have them talk things through within their small group around the table.

Just before you wrap things up, have each group select a table host or leader. You can do this by having everyone point at once to the person at their table they feel would best facilitate discussion for future meetings.

Ask those newly elected table leaders to stay after for a few minutes, and offer them an opportunity to be further trained as small-group leaders as they lead discussions throughout the course of the study.

Subsequent Weeks

Begin in prayer. Then give a short message (15-25 minutes) based upon the scripture used for that lesson. Pull out the most motivating topics or points, and strive to make the discussion relevant to the everyday life and world of a typical man. Then leave time for each table to work through the discussion questions listed in the curriculum. Be sure the discussion facilitators at each table close in prayer.

At the end of the eight sessions, you might want to challenge each "table group" to become a small group, inviting them to meet regularly with their new small-group leader and continue building the relationships they've begun.

prayer request record

Date:

Name:

Prayer Request:

Praise:

Date:

Name:

Prayer Request:

Praise:

Date:

Name:

Prayer Request:

Praise:

Date:

Name:

Prayer Request:

Praise:

Date:

Name:

Prayer Request:

Praise:

defining group roles

Group Leader: Leads the lesson and facilitates group discussion.

Apprentice Leader: Assists the leader as needed, which may include leading the lesson.

Refreshment Coordinator: Maintains a list of who will provide refreshments. Calls group members on the list to remind them to bring what they signed up for.

Prayer Warrior: Serves as the contact person for prayer between sessions. Establishes a list of those willing to pray for needs that arise. Maintains the prayer-chain list and activates the chain as needed by calling the first person on the list.

Social Chairman: Plans any desired social events during group sessions or at another scheduled time. Gathers members for planning committees as needed.

small-group roster

Name:
Address:
Phone: E-mail:

Name:
Address:
Phone: E-mail:

Name:
Address:
Phone: E-mail:

Name:
Address:
Phone: E-mail:

Name:
Address:
Phone: E-mail:

Name:
Address:
Phone: E-mail:

spiritual checkup

Your answers to the statements below will help you determine which areas you need to work on in order to grow spiritually. Mark the appropriate letter to the left of each statement. Then make a plan to take one step toward further growth in each area. Don't forget to pray for the Lord's wisdom before you begin. Be honest. Don't be overly critical or rationalize your weaknesses.

Y = Yes
S = Somewhat or Sometimes
N = No

My Spiritual Connection with Other Believers

____ I am developing relationships with Christian friends.

____ I have joined a small group.

____ I am dealing with conflict in a biblical manner.

____ I have become more loving and forgiving than I was a year ago.

____ I am a loving and devoted husband and father.

My Spiritual Growth

____ I have committed to daily Bible reading and prayer.

____ I am journaling on a regular basis, recording my spiritual growth.

___ I am growing spiritually by studying the Bible with others.

___ I am honoring God in my finances and personal giving.

___ I am filled with joy and gratitude for my life, even during trials.

___ I respond to challenges with peace and faith instead of anxiety and anger.

___ I avoid addictive behaviors (excessive drinking, overeating, watching too much TV, etc.).

Serving Christ and Others

___ I am in the process of discovering my spiritual gifts and talents.

___ I am involved in ministry in my church.

___ I have taken on a role or responsibility in my small group.

___ I am committed to helping someone else grow in his spiritual walk.

Sharing Christ with Others

___ I care about and am praying for those around me who are unbelievers.

___ I share my experience of coming to know Christ with others.

___ I invite others to join me in this group or for weekend worship services.

___ I am praying for others to come to Christ and am seeing this happen.

___ I do what I can to show kindness to people who don't know Christ.

Surrendering My Life for Growth

___ I attend church services weekly.

___ I pray for others to know Christ, and I seek to fulfill the Great Commission.

___ I regularly worship God through prayer, praise, and music, both at church and at home.

___ I care for my body through exercise, nutrition, and rest.

___ I am concerned about using my energy to serve God's purposes instead of my own.

My Identity in the Lord

___ I see myself as a beloved son of God, one whom God loves regardless of my sin.

___ I can come to God in all of my humanity and know that He accepts me completely. When I fail, I willingly run to God for forgiveness.

___ I experience Jesus as an encouraging Friend and Lord each moment of the day.

___ I have an abiding sense that God is on my side. I am aware of His gracious presence with me throughout the day.

___ During moments of beauty, grace, and human connection, I lift up praise and thanks to God.

___ I believe that using my talents to their fullest pleases the Lord.

___ I experience God's love for me in powerful ways.

small-group covenant

As a committed group member, I agree to the following:*

- **Regular Attendance.** I will attend group sessions on time and let everyone know in advance if I can't make it.
- **Group Safety.** I will help create a safe, encouraging environment where men can share their thoughts and feelings without fear of embarrassment or rejection. I will not judge other guys or attempt to fix their problems.
- **Confidentiality.** I will always keep to myself everything that is shared in the group.
- **Acceptance.** I will respect different opinions or beliefs and let Scripture be the teacher.
- **Accountability.** I will make myself accountable to the other group members for the personal goals I share.
- **Friendliness.** I will look for those around me who might join the group and explore their faith with other men.
- **Ownership.** I will prayerfully consider taking on a specific role within the group as the opportunity arises.
- **Spiritual Growth.** I will commit to establishing a daily quiet time with God, which includes doing the homework for this study. I will share with the group the progress I make and the struggles I experience as I seek to grow spiritually.

Signed: _____ Date: _____

---

* *Permission is given to photocopy and distribute this form to each man in your group. Review this covenant quarterly or as needed.*

about the authors

STEPHEN ARTERBURN is coauthor of the best-selling Every Man series. He is also founder and chairman of New Life Clinics, host of the daily *New Life Live!* national radio program, and creator of the Women of Faith conferences. A nationally known speaker and licensed minister, Stephen has authored more than forty books. He lives with his family in Laguna Beach, California.

KENNY LUCK is president and founder of Every Man Ministries, coauthor of *Every Man, God's Man* and its companion workbook, and coauthor of the Every Man Bible studies. He is the area leader for men's ministry and teaches a men's interactive Bible study at Saddleback Church in Lake Forest, California. He and his wife, Chrissy, have three children and reside in Trabuco Canyon, California.

TODD WENDORFF is a graduate of University of California, Berkeley, and holds a ThM from Talbot School of Theology. He serves as a teaching pastor at King's Harbor Church in Redondo Beach and is an adjunct professor at Biola University. He is an author of the Doing Life Together Bible study series. Todd and his wife, Denise, live with their three children in Rolling Hills Estates, California.

start a bible study
and connect with others
who want to be God's man.

Every Man Bible Studies are designed to help you discover, own, and build on convictions grounded in God's word. Available now in bookstores.

WATERBROOK
PRESS

every man's battle workshops

from New Life Ministries

new Life Ministries receives hundreds of calls every month from Christian men who are struggling to stay pure in the midst of daily challenges to their sexual integrity and from pastors who are looking for guidance in how to keep fragile marriages from falling apart all around them.

As part of our commitment to equip individuals to win these battles, New Life Ministries has developed biblically based workshops directly geared to answer these needs. These workshops are held several times per year around the country.

- Our workshops **for men** are structured to equip men with the tools necessary to maintain sexual integrity and enjoy healthy, productive relationships.

- Our workshops **for church leaders** are targeted to help pastors and men's ministry leaders develop programs to help families being attacked by this destructive addiction.

Some comments from previous workshop attendees:

"An awesome, life-changing experience. Awesome teaching, teacher, content and program."   —DAVE

"God has truly worked a great work in me since the EMB workshop. I am fully confident that with God's help, I will be restored in my ministry position. Thank you for your concern. I realize that this is a battle, but I now have the weapons of warfare as mentioned in Ephesians 6:10, and I am using them to gain victory!"   —KEN

"It's great to have a workshop you can confidently recommend to anyone without hesitation, knowing that it is truly life changing. Your labors are not in vain!"   —DR. BRAD STENBERG, Pasadena, CA

If sexual temptation is threatening your marriage or your church, please call **1-800-NEW-LIFE** to speak with one of our specialists.

every man conferences
revolutionizing local churches

"This is a revolutionary conference that has the potential to change the world. Thanks Kenny! The fire is kindled!"   —B.J.

"The conference was tremendous and exactly what I needed personally. The church I pastor is starting a men's group to study the material launched at this conference. This is truly an answer to my prayer!"   —DAVID

"Thank you! Thank you! Thank you! I didn't know how much I needed this. I look forward to working through the material with my small group."   —BOB

"It's the only conference I have attended where I will go back and read my notes!"   —ROGER

"This is a conference every man should attend."   —KARL

"After years of waffling with God, I am ready to welcome Him into my every day life. Thanks for giving me the tools to help me develop a relationship with God."   —GEORGE

"This revolutionary conference is the next wave of men's ministry in America."   —STEVE ARTERBURN, Coauthor of *Every Man's Battle*

If you want to :
- **address the highest felt need issues among men**
- **launch or grow your men's ministry**
- **connect your men in small groups around God's Word**
- **and reach seeking men with the Gospel**

Join with other churches or sponsor an every man conference in your area.

For information on booking Kenny Luck or scheduling an Every Man Conference contact Every Man Ministries at 949-766-7830 or email at everymanministries@aol.com. For more information on Every Man events, visit our website at everymanministries.com.

Printed in the United States
by Baker & Taylor Publisher Services